Paw Prints

German Shepherds

by Kaitlyn Duling

Bullfrog Books

Ideas for Parents and Teachers

Bullfrog Books let children practice reading informational text at the earliest reading levels. Repetition, familiar words, and photo labels support early readers.

Before Reading

- Discuss the cover photo. What does it tell them?
- Look at the picture glossary together. Read and discuss the words.

Read the Book

- "Walk" through the book and look at the photos. Let the child ask questions. Point out the photo labels.
- Read the book to the child, or have him or her read independently.

After Reading

- Prompt the child to think more. Ask: Have you ever seen a German shepherd? Would you like to play with one?

Bullfrog Books are published by Jump!
5357 Penn Avenue South
Minneapolis, MN 55419
www.jumplibrary.com

Library of Congress Cataloging-in-Publication Data

Names: Duling, Kaitlyn, author.
Title: German shepherds / by Kaitlyn Duling.
Description: Minneapolis, MN : Jump!, Inc., 2018.
Series: Paw prints
Series: Bullfrog books | Includes index.
Audience: Ages 5 to 8. | Audience: Grades K to 3.
Identifiers: LCCN 2017041188 (print)
LCCN 2017043179 (ebook)
ISBN 9781624967733 (ebook)
ISBN 9781624967726 (hardcover : alk. paper)
Subjects: LCSH: German shepherd dog—Juvenile literature.
Classification: LCC SF429.G37 (ebook)
LCC SF429.G37 D85 2018 (print) | DDC 636.737—dc23
LC record available at https://lccn.loc.gov/2017041188

Editor: Jenna Trnka
Book Designer: Molly Ballanger

Photo Credits: Eric Isselee/Shutterstock, cover, 1, 22, 24; Marcel Jancovic/Shutterstock, 3; Jennay Hitesman/Shutterstock, 4; Michelle Gilders/SuperStock, 5; Michael Ryno/Shutterstock, 6–7; dogist/Shutterstock, 8–9; purplequeue/Shutterstock, 10, 23ml; imageBROKER/SuperStock, 11; Elen11/iStock, 12–13, 23tl; Radius Images/Alamy, 14; Monika Wisniewska/Shutterstock, 15; Juniors Bildarchiv/Alamy, 16–17, 23mr; Africa Studio/Shutterstock, 18–19 (background), 23tr; ESB Professional/Shutterstock, 18–19 (boy), 23tr; gpointstudio/iStock, 20–21 (background), 23br; Erik Lam/Shutterstock, 20–21 (dog), 23br; justsolove/Shutterstock, 23bl.

Printed in the United States of America at Corporate Graphics in North Mankato, Minnesota.

Table of Contents

Smart and Strong

Look! A big dog.

What kind is it?

A German shepherd!

ears

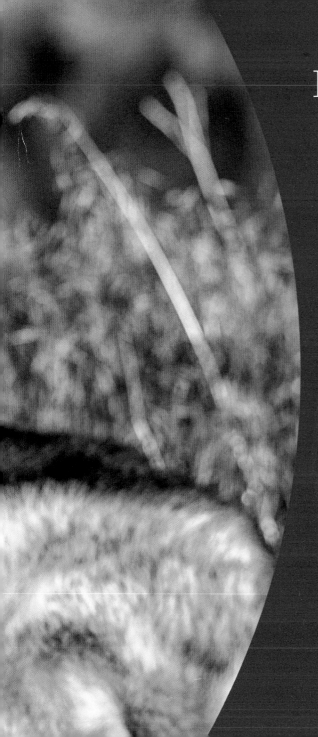

Look at its ears.

Big. Tall. Pointed.

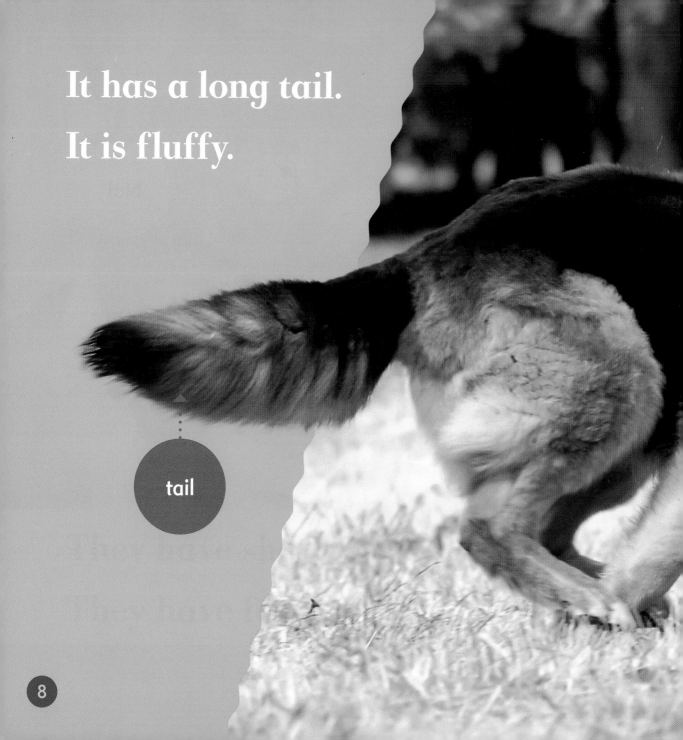

It has a long tail.
It is fluffy.

tail

The coat is long.

Many are black and brown.

But they can be other colors.

This one is white!

Where are they from?

Germany.

They were bred to work.

They are very strong.

This one works
with police.

14

It sniffs.

It helps find things.

15

What is this one?

A rescue dog.

It helps people.

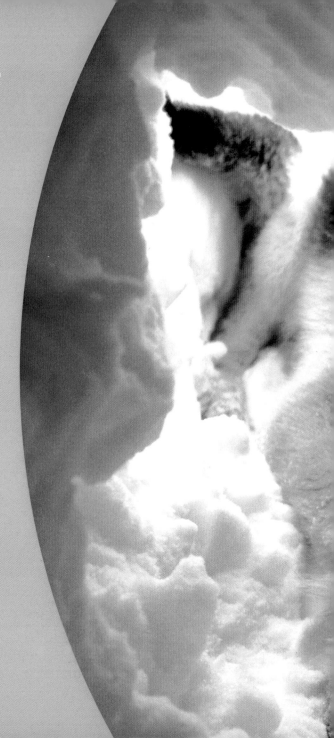

These dogs are very loyal.
They protect us.

German shepherds
love to work.

They are very smart.

Would you like
to train one?

A German Shepherd Up Close

ear

coat

muscles

tail

paw

Picture Glossary

bred
Developed as a dog breed.

loyal
Faithful.

coat
A dog's fur.

rescue dog
A dog that is trained to help find and rescue people.

Germany
A country in Western Europe.

train
To teach an animal how to do something.

Index

To Learn More

Learning more is as easy as 1, 2, 3.

1) Go to www.factsurfer.com

2) Enter "germanshepherds" into the search box.

3) Click the "Surf" button to see a list of websites.

With factsurfer.com, finding more information is just a click away.